Get a Life, Not Just a Job

By

Rob Collins

This edition (v2.1) published 17th February 2014

First published in February 2014 by Rob Collins

Copyright © Rob Collins 2014

Rob Collins has asserted his right to be identified as the author of this Work in accordance with the Copyright, Designs and Patents Act 1988.

All rights reserved. No part of this publication may be reproduced, stored in a retrieval system, or transmitted in any form or by any means, electronic, mechanical, photocopying, recording or otherwise, without the prior permission of the copyright owner.

All characters appearing in this work are fictitious. Any resemblance to real places, organisations, or persons (living or dead), is coincidental.

UK English -> US English Translations

This book contains many UK English terms and colloquialisms which may not make sense to our transatlantic cousins. Here's a quick translation guide.

UK English	US English
Rozzers	Police
Bollocks	Nonsense

Contents

Introduction 1

Chapter 1 – Why You Need to Get a Life 2

Chapter 2 – How to Un-Fuck Your Career 5

Chapter 3 – Set your GPS, Calibrate Your Compass 8

Chapter 4 – Choosing Your First E 12

Chapter 5 – Evalu-8 15

Chapter 6 – Make like Darwin and EVOLVE, Mother Fucker 17

Chapter 7 – Hints, Tips and Advice 22

Appendix 1 – Values and Anti-Values 25

Introduction

Ever since my first job, I've disliked the way typical corporations work. You're no longer allowed to be a person – you're just a stripped down employee, consigned to fulfil a particular role and nothing more. You get paid just enough to make you fairly comfortable, but not quite enough to *really* enjoy life. You're kept only as long as you're useful. Unless you're very lucky, your bosses don't actually care about who you are as a person, they only care that you're doing your job.

Lots of new graduates emerge from University starry-eyed, expecting the world to fall at their feet. They are now experts in their chosen field – at least they think they are. The trouble is, theoretical knowledge goes out-of-date so rapidly these days. And if you don't have much practical experience in your chosen field, you're next to useless to most employers, especially if you don't fit their narrow pre-conceived definition of an ideal employee. That's why so many graduates these days end up serving coffee in Starbucks. Though the free lattes often help to seal the deal.

But what if you didn't have to have a job just to pay your bills? What if you could have a job so awesome that you sprang out of bed every day, delighted to start work?

What if work didn't even feel like work at all (most of the time)? What if it felt like *play*?

Well, I'm here to tell you that it's not just an impossible pipe dream. You can actually make it happen.

Better than that, I actually have a methodology you can follow which really, genuinely, cross-my-heart-and-hope-to-die, honestly *works*.

Rob Collins

P.S. If you enjoy this book, please feel free to leave an honest review on Amazon.

Chapter 1 – Why You Need to Get a Life

Admit it, you hate your job. That's why you're reading this book, isn't it?

Those fuckers take you for granted, don't seem to be able to see your true worth. And the politics?! Fucking hell, they're enough to drive a man to distraction. Manager A fucking over Manager B just out of pettiness and an attempt to climb the greasy ladder of success? Fuck that.

Yes, I say 'Fuck' a lot. No, I'm not sorry.

So, how did you end up in this predicament? You're clever, you're talented, you're ambitious… yet somehow your job is draining the life out of you. It's good you picked up this book or you might have gone postal and murdered several colleagues with a staple gun (slowly – it takes a lot of staples to kill someone, not that I've tried… ***cough***) before taking your own life with a hole punch (which really is not easy – I've tried).

Spare yourself that pain – follow me instead. We'll get you back on a sane career path quick-smart.

Why your career is fucked - Reason 1 - Education

It's not your fault really. Our whole education system is still struggling to escape from a paradigm designed in the 19th Century designed to produce good little obedient workers for factories.

School is an automated production line in which you are slowly engineered into a robot with precise characteristics. It's a process which takes people from age 5 up to at least age 18. If you show particular aptitude in certain areas, you can train right up to age 21-ish and maybe even beyond that if you're ultra-nerdy and want to do a PhD.

Ironically, and perhaps appropriately, after you are created (don't forget that you're just a very sophisticated robot, programmed to think and behave in a certain way), you're dumped off the end of the conveyor belt into a massive pile of scrap called "The Unemployed".

Now your unholy task is to find a career for yourself... Via guesswork... Having never had a career before... Because your mind is brilliant at predicting what things will be like if you've never done anything like them before. Oh no, hang on, I'm talking utter bollocks. What a shit system!

Sure, if you're lucky you'll have done some work experience at school. If your education was quite vocational in nature, you may have even built up a few months of experience.

But hang on a second, fresh out of school, with little to no real experience, you're expected to choose a career that will last you the whole of your life? Suddenly it doesn't seem fair that based on 2 miserable weeks stacking shelves in a supermarket, you're now expected to make a decision that will dominate your life for 40+ years.

I don't know about you, but to me that's **fucking ludicrous**.

Why your career is fucked - Reason 2 – Corporations Are Evil

Long gone are the days where you could count on your multi-national employer to look after you for life. Let me tell you a little secret – corporations are evil.

Imagine you have a nasty Uncle. Some of you may not need to imagine. This Uncle is utterly selfish. Everything he does is with the intention of making as much money as possible. He doesn't share, not even with you, his only nephew. No amount of money is enough for him – he is obsessed with never-ending growth. One day you realise that even the nice things he does for people are actually engineered just to make him *look* nice, with the ultimate aim of taking more money from people.

He stamps on the throats of his competitors, gleefully destroying them and celebrating their demise. He has no real regard for rules or laws – if he thinks he can get away with breaking the law to make more profit, he will probably try it. He'll even try to change the law so some of his more dubious practices actually become legal.

He has no compassion, doesn't feel love, doesn't care about the world's problems. Heck – he doesn't even care about you, even though you dedicate 1/3 of your life to working your backside off for him. You're just a means to an end for him – a tool to be used in the never-ending quest to make ever more money.

Basically, your Uncle's a cunt. He's a sociopathic mixture of Sauron and Mr Burns from The Simpsons.

But wait a second, he's not your Uncle. No, he's actually a corporation masquerading as a nice person.

Welcome to our modern paradigm of capitalism and globalisation. When you think about it, it's kinda disturbing, isn't it.

Some Solutions

1) Select a corporation you particularly dislike and plot to blow up its head office. THAT WAS A JOKE! DO NOT ACTUALLY DO THIS! THIS IS INTENDED AS SATIRE & HUMOUR!
2) Don't worry too much about deciding on your ideal career up front, you can work it out as you go along.
3) In my opinion, working for yourself or joining an ethical small business is the way forward. I hate most corporations (as if you couldn't tell), but perhaps they'll suit you. Most people look to employment with a large corporation as their first resort. I'm suggesting you make it your last resort.
4) Do something you *like*, rather than something that pays well. Money isn't everything (said every poor person ever).
5) Cancel that Amazon order for home-made bomb components. I TOLD YOU IT WAS A JOKE!

We'll go into more detail on each of these steps in the following chapters. Which is a good job really, because if I put them before this chapter, you'd be quite confused. It's also a stylistic *faux pas* to stick your first chapter five chapters in. But hell, it'd make me distinctive at least.

Chapter 2 – How to Un-Fuck Your Career

I'm going to say some things in this book which might challenge your existing belief system. But I'm not on a mission to convert anyone to my way of thinking. All this shit is just my opinion. But for now, just humour me and play along with these mad ideas… you can email me if you have any particularly strong disagreements.

We're going to take lots of E. Because everyone knows that drugs are the answer to all of life's problems. (Legal Disclaimer: They aren't.)

Rather than get mashed on MDMA, we're going to follow a three-step process called E&E&E. But for the more drug-aware amongst you, I don't mind if you want to call it a triple drop.

Here's a very brief overview of the triple drop. We'll go into more detail in later chapters.

Step 1 - Your First E (Experimentation)

Your first E (in E&E&E) is always the best. OK, I'll stop with the drug references now (maybe).

The first E is called **Experimentation**. Sounds fun, doesn't it! Get your white lab coat and safety goggles, we're gonna blow some shit up (not really).

Basically, rather than trying to predict your ideal career up front, we're going to run a series of little experiments, seeing what works and what doesn't.

The theory behind this is that it's ludicrous to try to decide on your career when you've had next to no experience of what real jobs are like. Sure, being a Thompson holiday rep does seem like a laugh – you get to go on lots of free holidays to Greece and see lots of girls in bikinis. But when you're sweating your arse off in a shirt and trousers, dealing with a family locked out of their apartment whose toddler has just puked on you, you might just change your mind.

So, in this step, we're going to select our first experiment and then implement it.

I like thinking, in fact I find myself doing quite a bit of it. But I also quite like doing. The main problem with thinking is that it tends to get in the way of doing. I'm going to suggest we try to minimise the up-front thinking and crack on with the doing.

For an intellectual, I sure seem to like the vocational approach.

So, now we've chosen *and* implemented our first Experiment.

Step 2 – Look in the Mirror (Evaluation)

You've been coming up strong. You're ready for more. It's time to drop that second E. This one is called **Evaluation.** Head off the dancefloor and into the toilets. Take a good look in the mirror. Drop that second E.

What we're doing now is Evaluating our previous Experiment.

What was that first E like? Did we enjoy it? Or was it crap?

Step 3 – Go Darwin (Evolve)

After staring into that mirror for a while, you might notice funny things happening. For example, your head might turn into a cat's. That's right, you've **Evolved.** This is the third E of E&E&E. I hope you like your new whiskers.

(This clubbing analogy is being stretched to breaking point, but bear with me.)

Basically in this step we need to decide how to Evolve our E&E&E process. We need to take things to the next level.

If, as a result of our Evaluation, we decide the Experiment was good, we'll adapt its recipe and try to cook up an even stronger batch (i.e. an even more fun experiment).

If, as a result of our Evaluation, we decide the Experiment was crap, well then we go back to our supplier (our imagination) and start over at Step 1, trying to identify another suitable Experiment.

A point worth bearing in mind: You won't ever find your ultimate job and think "A-ha! This is it, I can stop experimenting now". Sorry. Instead, you'll find that your E&E&E process will last you for the rest of your life. Everything changes, nothing stays the same. Neither will you.

That's why you need to keep triple dropping E for the rest of your life. With a bit of luck you're going to be buzzing your nuts off forever, starting now. You lucky bastard.

Chapter 3 – Set your GPS, Calibrate Your Compass

This chapter will help you to prepare for your **E&E&E** process.

Imagine a very long car journey. At the start of it you're born. At the end, you kick the bucket (sorry). Around 20-30% of the way through, you hit your first major milestone – your first job.

Every few miles from now until the end of your journey, there will be many, many more of these milestones, conveniently located at a fork in the road. Each milestone represents some kind of Evolution in your journey.

Sadly, you bought a second-hand GPS from Dodgy Dave down the pub. It doesn't work properly and it has the post code of its previous owner etched onto the case. Ooh, that little rascal Dave.

The GPS can find your final destination (death) no problem. In fact it marks your destination with a little cartoon icon of the Grim Reaper. Cute.

Unfortunately, the GPS can't tell you ahead of time whether to go left or right at each fork in the road you'll encounter. And there will be lots of them.

Instead, you'll need to make a judgement call (Evaluation) each time you reach a fork in the road. Do you continue in this general direction and if so, does your next Experiment take you left or right? Or do you decide this leg of the journey has not been particularly enjoyable and there's a big Swamp of Eternal Doom ahead, in which case, you retrace your footsteps for a bit and try a different path.

Using a GPS in this way might seem like it'll be very time-consuming and frustrating. But embrace the confusion. Allow yourself to feel comfortable with not knowing all the answers. Instead of focussing on the end destination, why not enjoy the scenery? Doing so really puts you in the driving seat. You get to have total control over how your journey Evolves.

Fortunately, you also have a good old-fashioned compass with you. Each time you reach a junction, you can whip out your compass and see which way is North. It won't always be right, but it's way more reliable than random guesswork.

Now it's time to do some work (sorry).

Calibrating Your Compass

You need some way to pick your first Experiment. How the fuck do you do that? You're currently at a road junction with 47 thousand different roads you could travel on. It's very hard to tell which ones will be enjoyable from here – your can only see a few hundred yards forward at most.

I'll let you into another secret: Most people (including me) don't bother doing the exercises in books. That's why nothing changes for most people. Don't be most people. Get off your ass. Come on, this'll only take a few minutes*.

1) Skills & Dreams Audit

What are you good at? What would you like to be good at? Baking cakes? Telling jokes? Running very fast? Owning your own hand gliding company?

- Write down a list of 10 things you are good at. Don't analyse or judge them, just write them down.
- Looking at each one in turn, have a think about whether you'd like to do an Experiment in that area. Cross off the ones you definitely don't want to make a career out of.
- Now write down 5 skills or activities you'd always wanted to try, or wish you were better at. These are your dream skills. What would you do with your time if it was easy? What would you do if you had all the skills, money and other resources you could possibly need? Dream big.

2) Identifying What Drives You (Your Values)

What's important to you? Family? Money? Success? Hard Work? Pizza? Laziness?

1) Write down 5 things that are important to you. See Appendix 1 for a list of examples. These are your Values. There are no right or wrong answers. Save your analysing for later, just write down what pops into your head.
2) Have a think about *why* each value is important to you. What does that value *give you*? The answer to this question is often the *real* underlying value and you may decide to discard the previous one.
3) Re-order your list of 5 things in order of how important they are to you. Have the most important one at the top, the least at the bottom.
4) Now write down a list of 5 things you hate. Again, there's a list of examples in Appendix 1. These are your Anti-Values.
5) Re-order the list of concepts you hate so the most hated one is at the top. No, you can't put Justin Bieber on this list. Oh, go on then, he *is* a twat.
6) Often our Anti-Values can help to prompt us to identify other Values we'd missed. For example, if you listed Healthiness as an Anti-Value, you might want to include MacDonald's as a Value.

I must offer my deep apologies to my good mate and life coach Tim Brownson, whose Values process I have blatantly ripped off and bastardised. He's actually written an entire book about Values which goes into much more detail. I highly recommend you buy it if you'd like to find out more. It's called, "Aligning with Your Core Values". It's very good – I wish I'd written it.

3) <u>Environment</u>

Answer the following questions. Don't agonise over them, just write whatever comes into your head. Feel free to skip any that you really can't answer. You can come back to them later.

1) WHERE: What kind of environment do you enjoy working in? Indoors, outdoors, in an office, in a forest, in a library, at the local coffee shop, on top of a skyscraper?

2) WHY: Think about some of the best times you've had at school or work so far. What was driving you? What was your motivation? What was your PURPOSE?
3) WHEN: What time of day do you do your best work? Do you prefer 9-5? Or do you prefer lie-ins and staying up late at night?
4) WHO: What kind of people help you to do your best work? Do you prefer loud extroverts? Or do you prefer quiet intellectual types? Men or women? Old or young? Conservative or Liberal? Jocks, Geeks or Prom Queens?
5) HOW: When you think about your best work, what methods or processes were you using? Did you strictly follow a rulebook, or were you making things up on the fly? Where did your ideas come from? Did you need to do a lot of talking with peers/colleagues before you could start? Or did you just dive straight in? Did you do a spider diagram or task list to structure your work?

Again, there are no right or wrong answers. All we're trying to do above is give you some ideas to start playing with, stirring up those creative juices.

(* OK, I lied. If you did the above 3 exercises properly then it should have taken at least an hour, or possibly several. If it took you more than a day, you're taking it all too seriously. Chill out, man)

Using a combination of the **Skills & Dreams Audit**, **Values** and **Environment** identified above, we're going to get our Dr Who Sonic Screwdriver, point it at your answers and use magic to charge your compass with Mega Energy ™. Now each time you reach a Junction (having completed a leg of your journey, i.e. an Experiment) your compass will be able to give you a good idea of whether to go Left, Right or Backwards.

Done? Good job. That was hard work!

Or did you just skip over it? Shame on you. Get your ass back there and DO THE EXERCISES. Are you really in such a rush to reach the Grim Reaper? Stop and smell the roses, man!

Chapter 4 – Choosing Your First E

Choosing your first E (Experiment) can seem daunting. What if you get ripped off by a dodgy dealer? What if your body decides E isn't for you and you die writhing in a pool of your own vomit? Yeah, both of those things *might* happen when you Experiment, but rest assured they're very unlikely.

Ideally your first Experiment should be something small, something you can achieve in just an hour or two to get a feel for it.

You could sit on your ass thinking about this forever. But remember that thinking is the enemy of doing. You don't have to decide on the *perfect* Experiment. Just start *somewhere*. Give *something* a try.

Even if you do your first Experiment and decide it was crap, you'll still have learned something. That already puts you in a much better position than someone who is still sat on their arse thinking about doing something (maybe, one day).

Stop dreaming, start doing.

Carefully look at your responses to the 3 exercises in the previous chapter. Mull them over. Then, after you've slept on it, pick something, *anything*!

Do try to pick something which takes you out of your comfort zone, at least a little bit. If you end up doing something you've already done many times before, you're unlikely to learn very much from it.

Example

Skills & Dreams: I'd always fancied creating my own videogame, and I know a fair amount about computers, psychology and depression (don't ask).

Values: For me personally, I knew that **Fun** is very important to me. **Structure** is a high-priority Anti-Value, so I realised I needed to work spontaneously.

Environment: I knew I enjoyed working with creative people, though I also like working for long periods on my own (I'm quite introverted most of the time). I was happy to work on this idea part-time, in addition to my day job. I didn't have enough savings to just quit my job.

So, by combining my **Skills & Dreams**, **Values** and **Environment**, I decided for my first Experiment that I'd try to design a fun videogame about the experience of depression; that I would work from home whenever and however I felt like it. Yes, really. And yes, it was a lot of fun (mostly).

Your Turn

So, what do *you* want to try for your first Experiment?

Just pick something.

Do it.

Go on, stop reading now.

CLOSE THIS BOOK IMMEDIATELY.

I mean it.

I'm not telling you again.

You're really testing my patience.

I'll tell your mother what a naughty little bugger you are.

RIGHT, you asked for it. I'm getting the cane…

What do you mean, you enjoy it?

Chapter 5 – Evalu-8

Have you heard of the 90s electronic duo, Altern-8? If not, get your ass on YouTube, sharpish.

If you have heard of them, also get your ass on YouTube. Altern-8 are legendary and are always worth a re-listen.

I recommend starting here:
http://www.youtube.com/watch?v=2_bL0hFyslg
(**Altern 8 Activ-8 (Come with me) #altern8xmas**).

The creators of dance classics such as "Activ-8", "E-vapor-8", "Brutal-8-E", "Hypnotic St-8" and "Infiltrate 202" actually have nothing to do with this chapter, other than the fact I wanted to write Evalu-8 instead of Evaluate. So sue me.

By now you should have completed your first Experiment. If you haven't then fucking get back to it you skip-forwarding twat. Or, if you're really stuck, skip ahead to Chapter 7 for some tips which hopefully will help you get unstuck.

This chapter is all about the 2nd E – Evaluate.

How did your Experiment go? Did you enjoy it? What did you learn from the process? Which bits did you like? Which bits didn't you like? Did you manage to Experiment in such a way that you incorporated your Skills, Dreams, Values and ideal Environment?

Did you find yourself in a state of "flow" during your experiment? Did time seem to pass quickly because you were utterly absorbed in the task at hand? Or was it all a hard slog?

Do you need to update your **Skills & Dreams**, **Values** and **Environment** based on what you learned from your first Experiment? If so, do that now. You'll probably find you'll keep going back to these questions and revising them over the next few weeks and months. Don't worry, that's normal.

Was your Experiment so much fun that you'd even consider doing it for free? Or was it so unpleasant that you really don't want to continue along this path?

Above all, always trust your own gut instinct. Learn to listen to that quiet little voice inside – it's rarely wrong.

Example

I absolutely loved coming up with the concepts and design of my depression-based videogame. I had some awesome ideas, even if I do say so myself. I was really excited about them. Sadly, what I sat down to start programming the videogame, I absolutely hated it. I was reminded of being at University – by and large I loathed programming. OK, lesson learned.

I did actually learn plenty of positive things too. For example, I learned how passionate I am about psychology and videogames. I realised I could potentially be quite a good videogame designer (just not a programmer). I also learned that I massively enjoy working from home, especially with my favourite music playing.

Please Ignore the Following Paragraph

This completes the chapter on your second E, Evaluate. The previous sentence was redundant. So was the one previous to this one. And that one. And that one… (And so ends my shallow and unfunny attempt to bulk up this slim volume's word count).

Chapter 6 – Make like Darwin and EVOLVE, Mother Fucker

Forgive the gratuitous swearing in this Chapter's title. Or don't – be offended, see if I give a fuck (I don't).

Now we're at the proverbial fork in the road and it's time to take that third E and decide which way to go next. Let's EVOLVE. This chapter is sponsored by Richard Dawkins (not really).

The first question to ask here is: **Did you like your first Experiment enough that you want to continue with it in some way, shape or form?**

If yes, great! Now you just need to decide how to tweak your Experiment to improve it.

Go back to the list of questions in Chapter 3 and revisit your answers, newly armed with your first batch of hard-won experience.

I can already see you transforming from a soup of amino acids into the first single-celled organism. This will be the first time you've ever been called an amoeba where it's actually intended as a compliment. GO YOU!

So, what could you change in your next Experiment to make it even better? What little risks could you take? How else could you push yourself a bit further out of your comfort zone?

What got you really excited about your experiment? What captured your curiosity the most?

If you really disliked your first Experiment and don't want to continue with it, remember that's totally fine. You've learned something, namely that this Experiment was simply not your cup of tea. Believe it or not, that's great! Now you get to try something else completing different! Remember you're already miles ahead of the thinkers who are still sat contemplating what to do for their first Experiment.

So, it's time to start your next round of E&E&E. Go back to Chapter 3 and start Phase 2! Or if you're now on Phase 3. Or Phase 4. Or Phase 5…

...

… Or Phase 867,643,751 (P.S. You've probably done more Experiments than the Manhattan Project by now. You're probably also quite close to reaching that Grim Reaper on your GPS. Take a break, you've earned it. And don't trust that innocent-looking farmer with the mysterious-looking scythe.)

"The only way to fail is if you give up" – someone, somewhere, who I'm too lazy to Google.

Example

I decided to abandon the videogame about depression after sinking something like 20 hours into it and not getting very far. Never mind. It was mostly good fun and interesting, though I now know I'd rather stab my own eyes out than be a full-time programmer.

Instead, I decided to have a break of a few weeks to let the dust settle.

Then, out of the blue, I started wondering what it might be like if I started writing more. Maybe I could be a blogger or even an author.

The spark of my next Experiment was born.

This page intentionally left blank.

Except that some idiot just ruined my lovely empty page by writing the previous sentence.

And that one! And that one! ... Oh dear, here we go again…

THERE! – was it SO HARD to have a simple blank page? No, of course not.

OK, you can continue with your "book(let)" now. Go on, get on with it. I haven't got all day you know.

Chapter 7 – Hints, Tips and Advice

This chapter is full of various odds and ends which will hopefully help you on your E&E&E triple drop journey. Which hopefully won't end up with you getting pinched by the Rozzers or in hospital.

Right now this manuscript is at 4,330 words. Now it's 4,333… No, 4,334. God dammit.

Anyway, I'd quite like to get to 5,000 words. That feels like a nice round number. So like a self-conscious male model who got caught trying to show off in front of the girls by shoving socks into his pants, I apologise for the padding.

Recap

I've walked you through the E&E&E journey, which is a continual, never-ending cycle of developing your passions. There is no end-point. Rather, your task is simply to enjoy the journey. Smell the roses.

The first E is EXPERIMENTATION. You choose an Experiment and then implement it, based on your answers to a few questions about your **Skills & Dreams**, **Values** and **Environment**.

The second E is EVALUATION. You take a step back, take a look at your Experiment and basically decide whether you'd like to continue with it or not. Either way it's fine, provided you learned something about yourself in the process.

The third and final E is EVOLUTION. You choose how to develop your next Experiment based on the experience you gained from the previous one. And offer a salute to Darwin in the process.

And round and round you go, hopefully having some really fun adventures along the way. Imagine yourself inside a washing machine. No hang on, that sounds painful. And you'd drown.

Instead, imagine yourself as a green recycling logo with three arrows pointing to each other in a circle. Except sexier. That's right, you're now 3 sexy green arrows. You are sexy, aren't you? Yes, of course you are.

And you wondered what a 99 pence book could possibly do for you!

"Advanced" "Tips" (Terms and conditions apply)

- Just start with something. Who cares if you're not sure about it. Stop thinking, start doing. As Nike say, Just Do It.
- Find mentors / friends / supporters that you trust to help you in your journey. Failing that, buy a tramp a coffee and a sandwich on the condition that he pretends to be supportive while you ramble on about your inane little Experiment. He'll be really impressed, honest.
- This process will feel difficult, confusing and frustrating at times. Deal with it. Rome wasn't built in a day. Or if it was, I'd be calling that Cowboy Builders TV programme. Seriously though, this process is well worth sticking with. Trust me, I'm a doctor.
- If you're still struggling to get motivated, the following 3 questions might help:
    - What happens if it all goes WRONG? Realistically, if you try this Experiment and it doesn't work out, what will you do next? How will you cope? How will you recover? When you think about it, you'll often find that you don't really have that much to worry about.
    - What happens if it all goes RIGHT? Go on, allow yourself to dream. Imagine yourself becoming incredibly rich, powerful, successful, athletic… whatever it is that makes up your dream. Feels good, doesn't it!
    - What happens if you do NOTHING? Everything stays the same as it is now. Often this is the most motivating question of all. That's because life never stays the same – things move on. You'll maybe become increasingly resentful of your current job. You'll be wasting time. How many more years do you want to be doing exactly the same

thing anyway? Technology and businesses moves on – if you do exactly the same as you've always done, how long will it be until your employer decides it doesn't need you anymore and makes you redundant? Surely that's scarier than doing an Experiment.
- Don't worry about not knowing all the answers yet. Just have faith that as long as you keep going with this process, things will slowly start to become clearer for you.
- One of the best ways to motivate yourself is when you switch from thinking only about yourself and instead start to think about how you can help others. What problems are there in the world and how can you help solve them? When you approach life from this perspective, you'll be amazed at how quickly things can change.
- What are your unique quirks and traits? Don't suppress them to try to fit in. There's a very good chance that they are actually the very best parts of you.
- Your initial Experiments don't have to earn you any money. At the start you're just trying to find activities that you enjoy and want to pursue further. Just have faith that when you reach a certain level of competency, provided you're helping to solve someone else's problem or desire, then the money will begin to flow.
- Do you have to quit your job and leap straight into full-time experimentation? Of course not. Just stop watching so much boring TV and instead invest some time each week into developing your future. If you manage to find a way to earn some money on the side from your Experiments (and assuming your employer doesn't mind), that's often the best place to start for most people. With a bit of luck you'll eventually start earning enough money to quit your job and do your "Experiments" full time.

Look at that: over 5,200 words (on the 1st draft). No padding required. Aaaand, relax. Me, not you. You need to get your ass Experimenting! Get to it, there's no time like the present!

Appendix 1 – Values and Anti-Values

Values

Here are some example of values. Values are basically things that are important to you. You'll notice that many of them are personal characteristics. It's far from a complete list, though this should get you on the right track.

Family	Adventure	Friendliness	Success	Reliability
Honesty	Organisation	Connection	Money	Growth
Integrity	Tidiness	Winning	Security	Learning
Humour	Peace	Competition	Health	Ambition

Success and Money are two tricky ones – definitely dig down deeper to see what those two give you. Your answer is likely to be the *real* Value.

I've also not included Happiness, because I assume that everyone wants to be Happy.

Anti-Values

Here are some examples of Anti-Values. These are your biggest turn offs, things you avoid whenever possible. Sometimes it's simply easier to think about the things we don't like (Anti-Values) rather than the things we do like (Values).

Greed	Violence	Loud noise	Laziness	Poverty
Lust	Dishonesty	Rudeness	Procrastination	Lateness
Jealousy	Excessive Stress	Aggression	Smelliness	Selfishness
Anger	Ill-health	Dullness	Messiness	Arrogance

If you enjoyed this book, please don't forget to leave a review on Amazon.

About the Author

Rob Collins is a published author (obviously), blogger, IT geek, Team Leader at The Unlost.com and volunteer with the UK charity Samaritans.

He owes a great debt to Therese Schwenkler at TheUnlost.com, who helped develop many of the ideas that this book is loosely based on.

In fact, for some people, The Unlost's own E-Course, "From Confusion to Clarity" may be a much better match than this book. Therese is kinder, gentler, more patient and better looking than Rob.

I'd love to hear your thoughts about this book. I'd especially love to hear about your own Experiments and results.

Please do feel free to get in touch here:

daydreamblighter@gmail.com

www.ingramcontent.com/pod-product-compliance
Lightning Source LLC
Chambersburg PA
CBHW051827170526
45167CB00005B/2195